S0-CBQ-639

THE RIVER IS A REASON

Acknowledgments

The author gratefully acknowledges the following journals where the listed poems previously appeared, sometimes in different versions:

The Alembic, "(Who) Art in Heaven"
Apalachee Review, "Sooner" and "Early Spring"
Atlanta Review, "Landing"
Chaffin Journal, "Days of Grace"
The Cincinnati Review, "Heron"
Coe Review, "How Do You Keep a Dog"
Ellipsis, "In a Future Tense"
Fourth River, "Doubts About My Father"
Gulf Stream, "Ice on the River" (formerly "Not Another Poem About Looking Out the Window")
Harpur Palate, "Why the River"
Illuminations, "Anniversary" (formerly "Yahrzeit," nominated for Pushcart Prize)
The Jabberwock Review, "Waiting for You in the Lobby Bar" and "New Year's Morning"
Limestone Review, "Pathetic Fallacy"
Meridian Anthology of Contemporary Poetry, 2008, "Snow Angel at Starbucks"
Poet Lore, "Sacred Spaces," "White Ribbon," and "Storm Door"
RiverSedge, "Begins With"
River Oak Review, "Everywhere the Lake"
Robinson Jeffers Tor House Foundation News, Summer 2010, "Hall of Records"
Sacred Journey, "Basso Profundo"
Schuykill Valley Journal, "Fog"

South Carolina Review, "My Father Brings Jacques Cousteau
    Home for Dinner"
Spillway, "Afterthought"
The Spoon River Poetry Review, "Galileo's Telescope" and
    "Pumping the Bilge"
Whiskey Island, "Refraction"
Zone 3, "The River Once Again"

I am also grateful to the Virginia Center for the Creative Arts for
providing time and space for the preparation of this manuscript.

Thanks also to readers and mentors: Julianna Baggott, JoAnn
Balingit, Peter Campion, Alex and Kelly Castro, Barbara
Crooker, Jehanne Dubrow, Kim Garcia, Frank Giampietro, Jody
Gladding, Marcia C. Landskroener, Kelly Lenox, Sarah Maclay,
David McNaron, Erin Murphy, Paul Shepherd, Joan Smith,
Barbara Buckman Strasko, and Nance Van Winckel, and artistic
collaborators, Diane Landskroener and Marcy Dunn Ramsey.

Special thanks to my mother, Eloise English Davies, for support
and inspiration. And most especially to John Lang, for his love
and sustenance.

The title was inspired by a poem called "Weekend" in the
collection *Awayward* by Jennifer Krovonet.

"White Ribbon" is dedicated to the memory of James
Landskroener.

"Why The River" is dedicated to the memory of Dorsey Owings.

Contents

III. *Flood*

In Memory

Thomas Daniel Davies, 1914-1991

≈

Sandblast

"and behold, a great wind came across the wilderness"

First the roof, then the sky.
Upheaval, a fall-

ing. Daylight rushing night
into small

corners. One by
one we are reduced

to our elements—fine
grit and the smell

of sulfur. Limbs
tumble. Less and

less. Dry-eyed, we can-
not blink. The desert

inside us now, we
must not blink.

I.

Ebb

Anniversary

How to begin again, here at the end?

The night sky, lingering into morning,
expels its cooler autumn breath.

Under the back-lit bridge, the river's blue runs past me.

I have forgotten all the prayers except
the hum of marshgrass—so I take the boat downriver, cut

the engine and drift across the stretch where your ashes must
    have settled.

Without stone or candle, I just want to feel your absence tap the
    hull.
But a large boat rocks me in its wake. Two jet skis rooster-tail.

The world is a noisy place, I tell you.

Slowly the tide refuses me, turns my drifting boat
around. So I throttle up and leave you

one more time in a silver V
of ever-widening wave.

Sighting

Straight down into
a flock of birds, it plunges—

solitary force, dark torso,
white head and tail:

it has to be an eagle.

Gulls barking, rising at the end
of the dock. Cormorants stitching

stirred-up water with their needle necks,
diving, disappearing,

reappearing in frenzied waves
of bait fish running.

I reach for the well-worn field guide
to confirm the scene and find

a careful annotation, dated
twenty years before:

Golden Eagle, upper Chester,
February 12

Another day, a different eagle
hovers. I add my own note:

Bald Eagle, upper Chester,
January. Cold.

Slides from the Attic

Myself before I knew I had a self or she
knew me—at two, still separate. One

placed atop a lawn chair watching fireworks.
Here, trying to brush her hair. Here, clutching

the neighbor's cat by the neck. The Other,
somewhere beyond the camera

maybe napping in that shadow stretched across
the grass or clasped inside those

tiny hands so sweetly
laced in bedside

prayer—just there,
killing time.

Storm Door

What I remember is the storm door's refusal to give
and then glass slicing the sky as my arms flew through it

(like Supergirl, I thought, who doesn't know
her own strength). Without pain or fear—

except on the face of a neighbor who stepped
through her hedge, still holding up clippers—

my mother screaming my father's name, a towel,
the car—a convertible—all converging as I sped by trees and
     telephone poles

to a hospital room and a metal bowl of frothy water.
Someone said *Please put your hand in here* and instantly

the world turned red. *I'm sorry*, I said,
because I had ruined the water. *I'm sorry*, I said,

for the glass on the doorstep, the clippers agape on the lawn.
I'm sorry, I said, and took back my hand. Now ancient and pale,

it had disowned me. What I remember is the way the flesh
left the bone where the wound between two

fingers puckered and how the inside flowed
out and how the outside rushed in.

How Do You Keep a Dog?

Wisdom: "The soul's natural food."
– Jacob Anatoli

She treed raccoons and maybe killed
a neighbor's goat. An outdoor dog,

you said. Dangerous, I said. And yet I came
to love her. Long before your shadow

fell, Molly began to stumble. I put her
in my car and drove her through the marsh

with the window down so she could snap
at the rush of seasons.

Today, a friend asked about her neighbor's lab:
How do you keep a dog from killing chickens?

I knew what you would say, if you were here to say it:
Tie the corpse around its neck and let it rot.

Never mind that it didn't work,
that you came home to find an empty twist of rope

around her throat: she'd eaten everything —
except two twigs, the chicken's feet

still dangling.

Widow

A woman defined by what she
lacks.

There are no words we say
and say.

A short line at the end of a
paragraph.

The River Once Again

Maybe a hundred boats bobbed
    under a sky that never
        would produce the fireworks
    we had come to see,

nor the boy, already gone before
    the searchlight's orbit—

one glowing spot of water,
    circling.

Each of us stunned in turn
    as we gripped the gunwale and
      rocked in the wake
    until the helicopter
        shuddered off to darkness.

Before one motor—then
    another—would
start and rev and turn,

it was the silence
    we'd all remember—
      our unwillingness to
        break it.

What Scares Me

Not the ice on the river
solid a week now

under fresh snow turned back
like bedsheets

but my own warm breath,
the thaw, a sudden

plunge, then rising
to find what was

beneath is now above,
a sky of stone, no opening.

Snow Angel at Starbucks

Right in the middle of you telling
me of your mother's sudden
death, I remember that I dreamed
I bought a Buick.

The only free table is the high one in
the window, so we perch
on thin wire stools while snow
fills the sky beside us.

Your fingers huddle by the steaming
peaks of froth. You twirl a tiny spoon
to rearrange its crust.

Thank God—I think—
a dream.

We blow in our coffee and it breathes
back at us. A warm insistence.
A silhouette.

Landing

Like driving off a bridge—we always think
about it, never do it—but what if we did
just once, breaking through those Jersey barriers,
shattering concrete, sparks fleeing the tires

like birds startled from their nests, guard rail
splintering, brake and accelerator both
gone dumb without the ground to hear them,
wingless flight—it can't be pretty—awkward

as a child's first somersault, turning head and
feet around and landing—

well, there is no landing, they say you never land
in dreams—or if you did, you'd die—
so you just keep churning air and bracing
for the end and wondering if the world will toss
its objects after you.

That's how it feels to drag my legs across
the bed and slide them
to the floor.

Ice on the River

Nothing moves this morning.

Even where the channel cuts
the deepest, the water is a silver
field of rows and ridges
holding still.

Inside, the furnace hammers
on a labyrinth of pipes to keep
hot water racing through them—
contracting,

expanding, as the river's edges blister
by the pilings of my dock.

Long Before the Wheel

There was the shoe.

You can trace the evolution of our soles
    by the way they pressed themselves

into the meadow grass or wore
    away the marble steps with one day

scraped against another. Plaited grass
    and bark, then leather hides and now synthetics.

Sharp and purposeful or rubber-
    wedged and sporty, the shoe will walk us

down the block to get the paper, hustle
    us through airports, take us straightaway

to China, Istanbul, or Little Rock, and always,
    finally, home again.

And what you see when you look
    down may hint at where you'll go before you

sleep. Please note that no one sleeps in shoes.
    Even sleepwalkers must pick their way

on bones and calluses
    across the dream that's underfoot.

Power Failure

No light in the library—

leather bindings hold
dust in the dark

The clock stabs the room
with zero after zero.

I dream I drive my car through
yellow flowers.

If Not

this morning, some morning

the squealing tires will catch the dog of my heart
at a blind intersection

the car, racing north
the dog, on the zig-zag

trail of irresistible scent—they are bound

to meet, if not
this morning, some morning.

Heron

Gray shape-
shifter, echoed
in a silver
river, some-
times looping
down in
question,
sometimes leaning
into fog—
a slash,
and now
a straight-up
exclamation,
hurrying a
fish along
its impossible
gullet. So
thin it's
a stick
in the still
tide—an I—
until
the neck
ripples,
the deed
done,

and the wings
unfurl in a giant
W, as the world
resumes its
ancient Work.

Interval

You count from here, my father
said, and touched the key
whose chipped lip looked like
my fingernail. Middle C

was how I found the other
notes. The D next door,
the E that sounded right
just after C before

the G, *My dog has*— C—
but this time high, a reach
for *fleas*. Hand over hand
my father guided each

departure and return
to show me how the song
would always find its way
to the tonic. Strong

measures. Silence and the urge
to mend a broken chord.
My father gone. The piano
out of tune, ignored.

I will go back, I say
to no one but the old
dog. Half-step. Half-step. Wait
for the cadence to unfold.

Drift

A veil of mist blends sky and
    roof and trees and everything that
        softly hums across

the water in a windless
    hour before the sun—which never
        really rose—goes down.

This is the weather of sleep.
    The calm that says there will be
        no storm, only the tide's slow sip

at the shoreline. What light
    is left curls up in the sky's
        gloved palm, sliding

sideways toward its final
    gesture. The river is a reason,
        if you need one.

New Year's Morning

The wind has sent the river
        away, revealing a canal that carves through crater

from the channel to my dock—the scar an engine
        left, churning homeward on a falling tide.

The wind, too, has mostly gone, leaving sycamore limbs
        that lost their hold during the night.

One still dangles
        in its last grip of branches, a Y which points and

sways in precarious survival to divine
        the new year: *Water has been here*, it says,

and will surely return. A promise I might believe—
        at least for now—if only those

loose limbs were not called
        "widow-makers."

Mudflats mirror pink from someplace behind me
        where the sun must be rising.

Migration

Mist rising off the water

as sunrise ignites
the marsh grass.

Mist tumbling
downriver in strands and

tangles, hurrying
to go

someplace
gone

II.

Slack

Day of the Dead

It started when the cannon fired a ceremonial
      burst. Windows shook. The sycamore dropped

another leaf and a dog on the riverbank danced
      around its master.

It started when I saw the wheels of birds churn
      sideways as they spun across gunmetal skies.

The sun, heavy and slow, just set.

It started when a whistle sounded from abandoned
      tracks and the air was spiked with embers. Stones

shifted in their gravel path.
      Black walnuts hit the roof.

It started when I found the hand that pulled the shade
      was just the memory of a phantom limb,

fingers given over to the absences
      between them—the multitude of things

they could not hold. I felt the gravity
      of mercy, the benevolence of flight.

It started when the hours began to take and
      take and give back only night.

Doubts About My Father

I used to wonder if my father was an imposter.
Where did he go each day in his dark suit and perfect shirt?
Was he running rum or gambling or even robbing
banks—wasn't he good with numbers?

How could a person disappear each day from eight
to six and not be up to *something*?

But when he dropped his briefcase and we sat out back
on a concrete bench and the evening held us both,
while katydids performed their Chinese opera, I knew
he was the real thing—a god without a heaven,

only a house, gathering shade and shadow, each room
reverberating like the soundboard of an old piano. One note
ringing still in the half-light.

(Who) Art in Heaven

The projectionist who reads the paper
in his booth doesn't care

who gets the girl in the end. He lingers
over a late supper—

chases peas around his plate
with stained utensils. Because

time has someplace to go,
the final reel, untended, ticks away

in blind orbit.

My Father Brings Jacques Cousteau Home for Dinner

More potatoes? Mother asks. *Oui,*
s'il vous plait, Cousteau replies as he stabs
his fork into another piece of steak.

We never miss your show, my sister
says, and sweeps her dinner roll across
the plate. *Vraiment?* Cousteau looks up.

He waves the fork of skewered meat
as if conducting every syllable: *Then I must ask,*
he goes on, *who is your favorite on the Calypso?*
Is it my handsome son, Phillipe?

Forks around the table stall. *Why no,*
my sister says: *it's you.* And forks resume.

Later, my father pours Cousteau another glass
of wine and tells him about a leak in the swimming pool.

Much later, Phillipe will die in a diving accident.
And later, no accident, my father.

We all sip black coffee.

Clockwise

They wait. They take his hand
as if to steady him against

a final rush, each minute
falling, rising, in its trip

around the clock. They wish
his death would never

come. Come faster.
Like the dance he shared with

the girl who would become
his wife, the step and

sway, the clasped fingers,
touch of palm to small of

back, the bright anticipation of
shadows as he brings her

close then lets her swirl away.
We wait. We hold our

magazines, turn pages, put
them down.

Begins With

My mother's stroke has left her struggling
for words: *Mexican, Mexican,*

Mexican, on top
of ice cream, turns out to be Kahlúa.

A *telephone* that *won't get channel eleven*
is a remote that won't respond

to frantic button-pushing—battery
dead or dying, I suppose. She can't tell

me that her mind is leaving both of us

behind, nor where it's going—no words, no
words for that.

Just a phantom space

in every sentence—gap-toothed—two
syllables, two

syllables, begins with _____.

In for a Penny

I placed it there on my way to
school, right where the rails crossed

our driveway. A breeze brought
pine from the nearby woods.

We had picked blueberries there,
swatting back the brambles

until September intervened with
sharp pencils and stiff, blue

notebooks. I hurried on, though
my new loafers pinched, and soon

stood in line by the school room door
forgetting that I'd left

Lincoln's head
on the railroad tracks.

But late in the day, as I
hugged new textbooks to my

chest and hurried up the drive,
I returned to the spot to find

an oblong piece of copper, flattened,
smooth and featureless. I lay

a hand on one raised bar
and then the other. I tried to feel

the tremor, listened
for a far-off whistle or some other trace

of what could strike the iron earth.
I turned my head to scan the

tracks but only saw two rails, never
touching as they rounded

the world's edges, leaving me behind
a sliver of what was

changed completely by the weight
of a single day.

More Tests

My brother phones to say he has
some kind of mass they must remove.

For two more weeks we all pretend we
are not scared—his wife, his kids, our mother.

As if there is no shadow tying us to
separate fates: my brother,

me, the aging dog, the fickle cat, all
subject to the constant tests of bacon, coffee,

shower stalls, the objects we must
mediate to prove we are, in

fact, ourselves.

I wake to pain—jaw firmly clenched.

There is no cure, my dentist said, before
he made a plastic mold for me to

bite all night instead.

Everywhere the Lake
Champlain

Outside every window, surrounding every mountain road
it winks and whispers *winter* to the greener leaves of birch and ash.

In laps and whitecaps, it flows its steady arms around
our little boats and wooden cottages. Determined

to go nowhere, we pause mid-paddle to hear a loon cry

then return to lifting water
as the world around us flows beyond us, North.

Strange Comforts

Because *tom kha gai* is just another
kind of chicken soup—a healer—lemongrass
and galangal scent the kitchen's steamy air
with layers that are exotic but familiar.

When I was sick my mother read out loud
to me. I still recall *Rebecca*, how the rise and
fall of her inflection blended plot
and fever till I fell asleep.

Now my mother's eyes see only wavy
lines and shadows. She cannot read at all
but her voice still rises sweet and
sharp—too sharp, I notice as she

tries to gauge how well I've warmed the soup.
I know she doesn't really like Thai food—
just wants distraction from the grayness
of her day. I place a bowl beside her, swirl

cilantro in among the chicken bits. A squeeze
of lime, a ring of Siam pepper. With each
ingredient, a hint, a hurt, a possibility,
and then—sometimes—a consolation.

Refraction

So many summers since my father
sat beside me on a stone bench. A warm

night. We watched the pulsing stars at
the river's curve.

He tried to tell me about lights and navigation,
though I never understood *red right returning*—

because for it to work, you have to
know if you're coming or going.

Red sky at night, he said, on a different
evening, as we carried drinks

to the patio for another round of
explanations. And then just once—and never

again—it happened exactly the way
he said it would:

Silent, except the ice cubes' quiet
stutter in the gin while the sun bore its own

witness. I saw the lozenge burning where
the earth turns away from us.

Felt the density beneath, the bending
in the thinner, higher layers.

The upper limb, my father called it, right
before its final flex at the tip

of what is visible: a last scattering,
a blaze of green.

Galileo's Telescope

This wooden tube has survived four hundred
trips around the sun to land

in a display of early instruments.
Calculations etched on shiny brass in

rings of tick marks so that time and space
align themselves in a narrow cylinder.

The docent invites us to observe
what Galileo saw in various simulations

but what I see is the light in my father's study,
how it blazed around his desk. The antique

maps he bought from stalls in Florence
gathered near him, their strange tints

and hand-lettering, with serpents porpoising
through uncharted waters. I can hear him, too,

explaining the Latin in soft syllables, his
hands stroking the world to hold its edges flat.

Here in the museum, light and dust and
lenses reassemble history in the night sky.

Everything shifts and blurs, doubles, then comes
into view. *We are not the center of the universe,*

the exhibition signage tells us. A vision so
terrifying, we must again recant it, as we walk

from room to room, surrounded
by the radiance of long-extinguished stars.

Hall of Records

Somewhere in a strange city,
my father cradled me in one arm while
gesticulating to the man in charge of records:

a birth—to write it down.

He'd always said we should go back there.
As if it proved that once and far away
we'd been part of the same enterprise.

Ecco! the man had said, as he clambered
backward down the metal stair gripping
a leather volume.

We talked about it often—priced
the tickets—but never made the trip.

Somewhere in a city with two
castles, my parents are still in love.

Ledgers lean against each other in the dust.
On a wooden counter pages spread
against the spine to admit a foreign name.

Two men witness. One enunciating every
consonant and vowel as he engraves them

into air, the other dipping a pen in black
ink to scratch out a few more characters.

Somewhere in a strange city,
this is recorded.

On the Other Hand

Sunday morning, the Museum of Asian Art is mostly
empty as we wander from illuminated case to case.

*Thailand, Eighth Century: The Buddha is depicted
seated on a throne, performing a gesture of teaching
with his right hand. No one knows what his
left hand is doing.*

Beyond sealed windows, a festival has overrun
the Square. Children with painted faces race ahead
of parents. Some hold dogs on leashes. Others push
strollers across cracked sidewalks.

A man with a wooden paddle stirs a giant bowl
of kettle corn over an open flame.

Skirted tables billow in the wind.

Inside, the stone deities remain serene.
No one knows what the left hand is doing.

But we can wait.

Basso Profundo

If you don't stop listening, you can hear
the bottom of the silence, feel it

beneath the soles of your feet.
The baseline, from which all music springs:

the dance of particles in the sunlight, the counter-
point of objects and their shadows. A wave

too large for the small chambers of our ear
to hold: rocking, rocking.

III.

Flood

In a Future Tense

Today, all day, I will be Anne Boleyn.

You can't speak to me, I'll tell my friends:
I'm locked in a tower.

You can't sleep with me, I'll tell my lover:
I'm married to a man with rings the size
of England.

You can't frighten me, I'll tell the executioner:
My neck is long and the blade
is sharp.

What will go on, has gone on, goes
on as surely as my loosened hair will tumble
toward my waist.

End in Sight

The coldest morning of my life, I'm driving
Highway 89 when a truck flicks salt across

my windshield. The wipers make a frozen smear but
with a peep hole, so I keep on driving—squinting

through the solid streaks and thinking I'm okay,
until I round a turn and sun comes at me full force

at eye level. The brightest bright ignites my brain
with paper, bedsheets, picket fenceposts,

snowdrops, shooting stars: a horn blares—
I have crossed into another lane. *This is it*, I think.

And then, a shadow falls across me
as I turn another bend.

Sharon, VT, 4 Miles, the green sign says.

And in the blessed dark, I see
that I'm still somewhere

on this curving earth.

Sooner

Sooner or later, your body will desert you
for a younger woman. Who would not choose

the slim waist of promise, the blue eye that
can swallow the distance and still read the menu?

My teeth are telling lies to the gums that
surround them like a sagging sock, about their

plans to stick around and chew when by night they
grind their way to freedom.

The breasts that used to hold out for the gentle
hand—suffice to say it's sad to see them sink so low.

Yes, I'm angry. I rage. I plead. I polish and tweeze.
But the saddlebags are packed. The thighs

will take their leave while the knees are
strong enough to carry them.

What can I hold on to, if not these crumbling
bones? Put on your pointy shoes

and let's go dancing, I tell my feet. Make it a
slow dance and sway those hips before

they can refuse you. With every step my
trusty heart will do its best to keep the beat.

Twirl, dip, whisper sweetly to the old dog
in the moonlight: *later, later.*

On Pointy Shoes

Though I recognize the pointlessness
of pointy shoes—why add an inch or
two no toe could occupy?—I've come
to love them.

The way they stab each step
before you take it. Hungry—but
restrained, because you cannot
move too fast in pointy shoes.

They thrust you forward—
hold you back—until the world can
see that you've arrived
in useless elegance. Yes,
useless, pointless,

vacant in those angled toes, and
still you strut and
pivot, poised
(above some pointy heels)

to hear dust and beauty echo
in the tapping of your feet.

Fog

Geese, in the fog, glide past
the dark mass of dock, their subtle bob intent
on a single shore.

Egyptian heads, occasionally an ancient bark to
mark their clumsiness on land—all neck and
legs and wobble.

One rises, stretches wings above the flock and shudders,
then rejoins the rest as they resume
their mission: to be black

against this whiteness.

Pathetic Fallacy

How like me to hear my own sad breathing
in the pulse of the wind,

the whistle of my winter nose,
geese crying across the river.

Damp hair sits on my shoulders;
snow bows the boxwood.

How like me to see my reflection
in a window pane.

Even when I look at you
it's my own pulse skips and rises.

Waiting for You in the Lobby Bar

Suits and shirts and spotted ties pulse
in the light of a TV screen so close it makes
me blink and it blinks back.

Everyone watching—even the bartender, who's balancing
a tray of sweaty pilsners. All eyes fixed
on the game and the time remaining.

I'm just looking for your tan suede jacket.

Sleeves expose glimpses of gold on wrists reaching
for peanuts. Late and getting later. The screen
expands and pixelates the bar.

You and me in another series of near
misses. Fourth down.

Numbered jerseys jump and flicker across
the racks of empty glasses.

Days of Grace

These are the holy days
between the heated house of winter and
summer's electric chill, when
your own breath is the thermostat.

The days of waiting
to find out where you have to go
or if you'll go at all.

Beyond the window traffic sounds reverberate
like the final cadence in a cathedral:
Send us now into the world in peace,
these days and their remembrance.

Let every breath linger on the palate before

you let it go, this body of evidence,
this thin wafer of time.

Pumping the Bilge

Yes, the overflowing possibility of anything that fills
and can be emptied. A return

of things to rightful places. An elemental balancing—
the deep gurgle, like the river

clearing its throat. The solace of words
themselves: the engine well, the bilge, a purge.

The crazed fiddling of crickets that says it is August,
it is hot, it is almost over. The sweat that is my body's

contribution to the sky and river. The steady
roll and rise of the hull beneath my

feet as lines that stretch across a falling
tide pull tight to test its limits.

Afterthought

Like the ringing after cadence
when the bow lifts off the violin

and the room holds one last
breath of spruce and rosin—

silence makes its own music, louder
than the brush of fingertips, a sudden swell.

"Longing," in its origin means "to make long."

Turn out the light, and let us see
if we can stretch the dark until the morning din of

bird call and traffic fails
to wake us.

Sacred Spaces

This chair that curves its arms around me.

The cover of a paperback that yawns above its opening page.

The furnace rumbles on.

Between the cat and the window, a stretch of carpet that muffles jungle heart.

Between you and me, the din of wondering.

The days that close the gap.

Let nothing—let all this—come
between us.

White Ribbon

Two white tails of ribbon dance
from the rail of the bridge

where the boy went
over. No one knows why. Not

the girl who declined to come
on a late-night ramble, not

the friend who tried to hold him up
in the moon-split current.

As I run across the bridge each morning, I reach
to take a long white arm of ribbon, to wrap

the wind around my wrist before I shake it off
and let it wave me by.

Early Spring

This is the year I asked for—when I thought my life might end.

High winds rattle the Bradford pears.
A swirl of limbs and blossoms.

An osprey zigzags across the sky holding a fat perch nearly his size.

Turkey buzzards hop around a carcass on the sand. Wingtips spread
    like fingers, efficient heads so small and red they
        disappear into the viscera.

The sun warms, in turn, each concrete pillar as it makes a sundial of
    the bridge.

The mystery of birds: so many die each day, where
are the bodies?

Sky and water silver where the rowers slide their shell beneath the
    bridge.

An eagle crosses branch to marsh and back again, watching every
    ripple that marks its territory.

A river without wind or boat, just a narrow ridge of water where the
    current runs.

Sunlight paints the bridge Venetian gold.

This is the year I ask for—when I think my life might end.

Three cormorants fly low above the mirrored edge of water.

Wave

What I think is the sound of rain in shivering leaves
is not rain at all, but a swarm of small black birds who swoop

from nearby trees to take a turn at the water's edge,
each one tipping wings to fling the river

along its quivering head and back. A celebration, ritual—or some
    relief
from the long, dry summer. In rotation, every bird

performing the ablution and then racing back to a slender
limb, still bobbing from the last departure. As each one goes

another takes its place, sweeping past
the next in near mid-air collision.

What I think is the sound of rain turns out to be
a rhythmic relay, my own pulse,

a feather on the tide,
thunderous.

Why the River

because it is a body

because it rises in our sweat,
    marries our breath to the cold

because it spills light back to us
    and hoards our shadows

because it leaves when gravity insists
    but always comes back

because it traps the clouds so we can sail across
    both heaven and earth

because it carries our tears, swells
    with our salt

because it is a body

because it bears our weight

MEREDITH DAVIES HADAWAY'S previous collection, *Fishing Secrets of the Dead,* was issued as a First Book Selection from Word Press in 2005. Her poem, "Hall of Records," was selected by Mark Doty for honorable mention in the 2010 Robinson Jeffers Tor House Poetry Prize. In addition to publishing her poems in various journals, Hadaway is a frequent contributor of book reviews to *Poetry International.* She serves as poetry editor for *The Summerset Review* as well as chief marketing officer for Washington College, where she occasionally teaches as an adjunct instructor in English. She holds an M.F.A. in Writing from the Vermont College of Fine Arts.

Hadaway lives on the banks of the Chester River on Maryland's Eastern Shore.